Editor
Sara Connolly

Managing Editor
Ina Massler Levin, M.A.

Cover Artist
Tony Carrillo

Art Manager
Kevin Barnes

Art Director
CJae Froshay

Imaging
James Edward Grace
Rosa C. See

Publisher
Mary D. Smith, M.S. Ed.

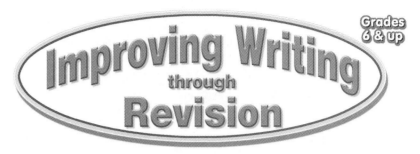

Grades 6 & up

Improving Writing through Revision

Author

Jessica M. Dubin Kissel, M.A.

Teacher Created Resources

Teacher Created Resources, Inc.
6421 Industry Way
Westminster, CA 92683
www.teachercreated.com

ISBN-1-4209-3859-9

©2005 Teacher Created Resources, Inc.

Made in U.S.A.

Table of Contents

Introduction

All writers revise. In fact, writers are constantly revising. They revise their initial ideas, their first drafts, each time they read their subsequent drafts, and they revise as they proofread.

Since revising is such an important part of the writing process, and we ask students to revise individually and with peers, it is important that we give students specific tools to use as they learn to revise.

Overview

Improving Writing Through Revision offers a simple teaching method that teachers can implement immediately in their classrooms to improve their students' writing and revision skills. Specific lessons are included in this manual, along with supporting materials.

Method

Improving Writing Through Revision builds skills throughout the year by adding a new skill each time the students reach the revision stage of the writing process. During the revision stage, the teacher introduces and models a skill, offers students an opportunity to apply the skill, reviews previous skills, helps students implement revision skills, asks students to reflect upon the revision process, and assesses students understanding of the new skill.

Implementation

Improving Writing Through Revision can be started at any point during the year and can be used immediately in any subject area where writing occurs.

Improving Writing Through Revision can be used in several ways. Teachers can follow the lessons in the order that they are presented in the book, present the lessons in a different order, use only selected lessons, or use only the method introduced in the book with individualized lessons. Included in *Improving Writing Through Revision* are

- Introductory Materials
- Nineteen Lesson Plans
- Assessment Items
- Lesson Extension Ideas
- Supporting Materials

Getting Started

This book is meant to be used in conjunction with the writing process. The basic steps of the writing process are prewriting, creating a rough draft, revising, editing and proofreading, creating a final draft, and publishing.

Upon reaching the revision stage of the writing process, introduce *Improving Writing Through Revision* to your students. Explain the importance of the revision process and the method that you will be using to help your students become experts in the revision process.

Each time your students have an opportunity to revise, you will be **introducing** and **modeling** a skill, having your students **apply** the new skill, **reviewing** and helping your students **implement** all of their revision skills, asking students to **reflect** upon the revision process, and **assessing** their usage of the new skill.

Students will keep their own growing list of revision strategies in binders, and whenever they come to the revision process, in any class, they can pull out their Revision Tools to help guide them. (See Materials, page 54.)

Since it is very time consuming to lead students through large writing assignments frequently, try to create opportunities for your students to revise their work. After students have written any multi-sentence response, present a new revision tool, and have students practice revising their work.

Many of the pages in the Supporting Materials section are designed to be discussion guides, and are therefore most effectively used as overheads. However, teachers who do not use overhead projectors can easily use the materials as handouts instead. Teachers should decide when it would be appropriate for their students to receive actual handouts, or when their students can use their own paper. Large chart paper or the board can also be utilized while completing the lessons.

A Guide to the Icons in this Book

The lesson plans in this book may include sample passages, skill checks, sample student responses, sample think-alouds, sample revisions, or activities. The text appears in boxes with icons in the upper-right corner. Each has its own icon to make it easier to identify.

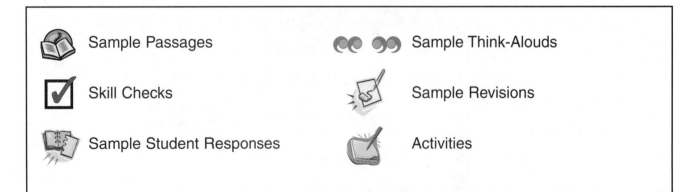

Sample Passages

Skill Checks

Sample Student Responses

Sample Think-Alouds

Sample Revisions

Activities

Writing Standards

Listed below are the McREL standards for Language Arts Level III (Grades 6–8).

McREL Standards are in bold. Benchmarks are in regular print. *The correlating lessons that meet each objective are in italics.*

- **Demonstrates competence in the general skills and strategies of the writing process.**

  Analyzes and clarifies meaning: *Lesson Fourteen*

  Makes structural and syntactical changes: *Lesson Three, Lesson Six, Lesson Sixteen*

  Uses an organization scheme: *Lesson Nine, Lesson Ten, Lesson Twenty*

  Uses sensory words and figurative language: Lesson Five, *Lesson Eleven, Lesson Thirteen*

  Rethinks and rewrites for different audiences and purposes: *Lesson One, Lesson Nine, Lesson Ten, Lesson Eighteen*

  Checks for a consistent point of view: *Lesson Four, Lesson Seventeen*

  Checks for transitions between paragraphs: *Lesson Fifteen*

  Evaluates own and others' writing: *All lessons*

  Uses style and structure appropriate for specific audiences: *Lesson Eight, Lesson Nine*

- **Demonstrates competence in the stylistic and rhetorical aspects of writing.**

  Uses descriptive language that clarifies and enhances ideas: *Lesson Five, Lesson Seven, Lesson Eleven, Lesson Twelve, Lesson Thirteen, Lesson Seventeen*

  Uses paragraph form in writing: *Lesson Nine*

  Uses a variety of sentence structures to express expanded ideas: *Lesson Two, Lesson Six, Lesson Sixteen*

  Uses some explicit transitional devices: *Lesson Fifteen*

- **Uses grammatical and mechanical conventions in written compositions.**

  Gathers and uses information for research purposes: *Lesson Fourteen*

  Uses simple and compound sentences in written compositions: *Lesson Six*

  Uses adjectives in written compositions: *Lesson Five*

  Uses adverbs in written compositions: *Lesson Five*

  Uses standard format in written compositions: *Lesson Nine*

These standards are used with permission from McREL (copyright 2000 McREL, Mid-continent Research for Education and Learning. 2550 S. Parker Road, Suite 500, Aurora, CO 80014. Telephone 303-337-0990.
Web site: **www.mcrel.org/standards-benchmarks**).

Lesson One

Improving Writing Through Revision, An Introductory Lesson

Objective
Students will understand the importance of revision as part of the writing process, and examine the *Improving Writing Through Revision* method of learning to revise.

Materials Needed
- Revision Tools (overhead, page 54)
- Personal Reflection Guide (overhead, page 55)
- Personal Reflection and Skill Check (overhead, page 56)

Build a New Skill

Introduce

1. Introduce or review the writing process. When authors write, they **prewrite**, create a **rough draft**, **revise**, **edit** and **proofread**, create a **final draft**, and attempt to publish their work in some way. Remind students that the writing process is not linear. Authors use these steps in a variety of ways as they write. For example, an author might begin to revise a rough draft, realize there is not enough information, prewrite to gather new ideas, revise the rough draft again, edit, begin the final draft, and decide that even more revisions need to occur. **Ask students to share successes that they've had with different parts of the writing process.**

2. Explain that learning to use each stage of the writing process will improve their writing. Then, explain that you will be giving students specific tools, or skills, that they can use during the revision stages of their writing. These are tools that students will be able to use whenever they write, in or out of school, this year or in the future. Explain that revising is a critical part of the writing process. It is the revising step that turns a good piece of writing into an excellent piece of writing. For example, during the revision part of the writing process, details are added that make characters and places come alive in readers' minds, dialogue is polished, repetitive words are deleted, and unclear comments are rewritten so that they become clearer. While authors struggle to get their ideas down during the rough draft, the revision stage allows authors to polish their work and focus on the detail of their writing.

3. Describe the method that you will use each time you introduce new tools for revision to the students.
   A. Explain that you will begin by **introducing** and **modeling** a skill, and having your students **apply** the new skill.
   B. Display Revision Tools (overhead, page 54) to the students. Explain that each time you introduce a new skill in class, students will use this handout to keep their own lists of the tools that you've taught. Whenever students revise their writing, they can reference this handout to help guide them.
   C. Explain that you will **review** and help your students **implement** all of their revision skills.
   D. Display Personal Reflection Guide (overhead, page 55). Explain that after the students have had time to apply their revision skills, they will **reflect** upon the revision process. Students may use these sentence starters to help them with their reflections, or they may compose their own reflections.
   E. Finally, clarify that you will **assess** students' usage of the new skill in the form of a Skill Check.

4. Continue on to your first revision lesson.

Say "Said" Sixty Ways

Objective

Students will descriptively state how a character intends to deliver dialogue.

Materials Needed

- Revision Tools (overhead and/or handout, page 54)
- Say Said Sixty Ways (Sample Passages A and B) (overhead and/or handout, page 57–58)

- Personal Reflection Guide (overhead or handout, page 55)
- Lesson Two Skill Check (overhead or handout, page 75)
- Personal Reflection and Skill Check (handout, page 56)

Build a New Skill

Introduce

1. Explain to students that writers try to create their characters so that they seem like real people. Ask: **What are different ways that an author might try to make a character seem real?**

   Answers will vary. For example, to make a character seem real, authors might describe the appearance of a character, give the character a name or an age, or have the character act in realistic ways.

2. Point out to students that one way authors try to make characters seem real is to give their characters voices. To do this, authors give characters dialogue. But, having characters "say" their lines becomes boring. Authors can make dialogue more interesting and more realistic by describing how characters deliver their lines.

3. Explain to the students that when they select a word to replace the word "said," they might be changing the meaning of the text. For example, there is a large difference in meaning between the word "said" and the word "screamed."

Model

1. Display or distribute Sample Passages A and B to the students. Read them aloud.

Sample Passage A

"What do you want to do today?" said Sam.

"I don't know. Maybe we can go rollerblading in the park," said Ceil.

"I hate rollerblading," said Sam.

"Okay, so what do you want to do today?" said Ceil.

Sample Passage B

"What do you want to do today?" asked Sam.

"I don't know. Maybe we can go rollerblading in the park," suggested Ceil.

"I hate rollerblading," muttered Sam.

"Okay, so what do you want to do today?" retorted Ceil.

Say "Said" Sixty Ways *(cont.)*

2. Tell students that Sample Passage B is the better passage because the word said is replaced with different words. Ask: **Why is it more effective to use a variety of words instead of using the word "said"?**

   Answers will vary. For example, when a variety of words are used, the writing is more interesting, it is more realistic, it allows the reader to learn things about the characters by examining how they speak to each other, and it's more descriptive.

3. Distribute Say "Said" Sixty Ways (handout, page 58) to students. This handout lists sixty words to use instead of the word "said." Remind students that there are many additional words that can be used as well. Encourage students to keep a list of their own ideas on the back.

Use the Tool

Apply

Remind the students that they will not always be able to use their new revision skills immediately, and they might not be able to use each of their revision tools for every piece of writing. But, they should consider each of their tools every time they revise.

Ask students to try to apply their new skill to their own writing. As students are working, walk around the room offering suggestions, monitoring understanding, and clarifying concepts. Then, ask the students to share some of their revisions.

Reinforce Previous Skills

Review and Implement

Ask the students to take out their list of Revision Tools (overhead and handout, page 54). Instruct students to add the new skill onto their lists while you do the same on your copy.

Use more descriptive words instead of the word "said."

Then, review the other revision skills that are on the list. Give students time to revise their work, considering each revision tool that they have. (Sometimes, you might ask the students to revise in pairs or in small groups, as well as revising individually.)

Seal it Together

Reflect and Assess

1. Have students complete the Personal Reflection handout (page 56) to reflect upon the revision process. For guidance, students can refer to the suggested sentence starters on the Personal Reflection Guide Skill Check (overhead or handout, page 55). Or, students can create their own reflections.

2. Then display or distribute the Skill Check for this lesson. Have students complete the Skill Check to assess their ability to use the new revision tool that was introduced. Students should write their answers on their Personal Reflection and Skill Check handouts.

Say "Said" Sixty Ways *(cont.)*

Skill Check

Revise this passage by replacing the word "said" with more descriptive words.

"It's really raining outside," said Anna.

"I know. I was planning on going outside," said Charlotte.

"Maybe we can find something interesting to do inside instead," said Anna.

---

3. Collect and review the students' work. You may opt to grade the work.

Sample Student Response

"It's really raining outside," remarked Anna.

"I know. I was planning on going outside," whined Charlotte.

"Maybe we can find something interesting to do inside instead," suggested Anna.

Extension Ideas

- Show the students how to add adverbs to these words to make them even more descriptive. For example: suggested *kindly*, whined *loudly*, or remarked *disappointedly*.

- Replace different words for the word said in the same piece of dialogue. Have students act out these lines to show how the meaning of the dialogue would change as different words were selected.

Vary Ways of Writing Dialogue

Objective

Students will vary ways of writing dialogue.

Materials Needed

- Revision Tools (overhead and/or handout, page 54)
- Sample Passages A and B (overhead and/or handout, page 59

- Personal Reflection Guide (overhead and/or handout, page 55)
- Lesson Three Skill Check (overhead or handout, page 75)
- Personal Reflection and Skill Check (handout, page 56)

Build a New Skill

Introduce

1. Create an overhead and display Sample Passages A and B, or distribute your handout.

Sample Passage A

"What's going on here?" asked John's mother.

"We were trying to bake a cake, but the cat knocked over the cake mixture," re-responded John's friend, Sam.

"Where is the cat now?" wondered John's mom, aloud.

"Oh, the cat is fine! He is outside licking his paws and having a snack at the same time," laughed Sam.

Sample Passage B

John's mother asked, "What's going on here?"

"We were trying to bake a cake," responded John's friend, Sam, "but the cat knocked over the cake mixture."

"Where is the cat now?" wondered John's mom, aloud. Sam laughed. "Oh, the cat is fine! He is outside licking his paws and having a snack at the same time."

2. Ask: **What is the difference between the two sample passages?**

   The speakers are identified in different locations in the first and second sample passages.

   Show students that when writing dialogue, the speaker can be named before the dialogue is written (John's mother asked, "What's going on here?"), in the middle of the dialogue ("We were trying to bake a cake," responded John's friend, Sam, "but the cat knocked over the cake mixture."), or after the dialogue is written ("Where is the cat now?" wondered John's mom, aloud.). Also, the speaker can be identified in a separate sentence from the actual dialogue (Sam laughed. "Oh, the cat is fine! He is outside licking his paws and having a snack at the same time.").

   Ask: **Why might an author choose to vary the place where the speaker is identified?**

   Writing becomes more interesting when the author chooses to vary the place where the speaker is identified. Writing begins to sound repetitious when the speaker is always identified at the end of the dialogue.

Vary Ways of Writing Dialogue *(cont.)*

Model

Write the following sentence on the board: **"Hi, how are you?" said Mary.** Then, Think-Aloud to model the new revision skill, or ask the students to help you revise the sentence. Here is a sample think-aloud.

> ### Sample Think-Aloud
> This sentence is correct the way that it is written, but I want to try to revise the sentence to make it more interesting. There is more than one way to revise this sentence, but I am going to choose to put the speaker in the middle of the dialogue. I am going to revise the sentence like this. (Model the revisions on the board.) "Hi," said Mary, "how are you?"

Use the Tool

Apply

Remind the students that they will not always be able to use their new revision skills immediately, and they might not be able to use each of their revision tools for every piece of writing. But, they should consider each of their tools every time they revise.

Ask students to try to apply their new skill to their own writing. As students are working, walk around the room offering suggestions, monitoring understanding, and clarifying concepts. Then, ask the students to share some of their revisions.

Reinforce Previous Skills

Review and Implement

Ask the students to take out their list of Revision Tools (overhead and handout, page 54). Instruct students to add the new skill onto their lists while you do the same on your copy.

Consider where the speaker is identified. Speakers can be identified in front, in the middle, or after the dialogue. Or, speakers can be identified in a separate sentence.

Then, review the other revision skills that are on the list. Give students time to revise their work, considering each revision tool that they have. (Sometimes, you might ask the students to revise in pairs or in small groups, as well as revising individually.)

Vary Ways of Writing Dialogue *(cont.)*

Seal It Together

Reflect and Assess

1. Have students complete the Personal Reflection and Skill Check handout (page 56) to reflect upon the revision process. For guidance, students can refer to the suggested sentence starters on the Personal Reflection Guide (page 55). Or, students can create their own reflections.

2. Then, have students complete the Skill Check (overhead or handout, page 75) to assess their ability to use the new revision tool that was introduced. Students should write their answers on their Personal Reflection and Skill Check handouts.

Skill Check

Revise this sentence by placing the speaker in another location.

"I wonder what the weather will be like this weekend," mused the child.

3. Collect and review the students' work. You may opt to grade the work.

Sample Student Response

"I wonder," mused the child, "what the weather will be like this weekend."

Extension Ideas

- During the editing stage, introduce correct ways of punctuating dialogue.

- When students are reading a story, have them examine how the author introduced speakers in his or her dialogue.

Know Your Narrator

Objective

Students will purposefully select a narrator.

Materials Needed

- Revision Tools (overhead and/or handout, page 54)
- Sample Passage A and Sample Revisions (overhead or handout, page 60)
- Personal Reflection Guide (overhead, page 55)
- Lesson Four Skill Check (overhead or handout, page 75)
- Personal Reflection and Skill Check (handout, page 56)

Build a New Skill

Introduce

1. Ask: **How could different people witness the same event, yet retell the event differently?** *Different people may interpret events differently, notice different things, or find different points to be important.*
2. Explain that just like different people retell stories differently, different narrators will tell the same story differently as well. **A narrator is the person telling the story. The narrator may or may not be a character in the story.**
3. Explain to students that authors must select who is going to tell the story. There are three basic ways that an author can choose to tell a story. Authors can tell the story in first, second, or third person.

   A. First Person: One of the characters tells the story. (I walked into a room filled with people, but I did not know anyone.)

   B. Second Person: The story is written as if it is happening to you. (*You* walked into a room filled with people, but *you* did not know anyone.) (Note: This method works best when an author really needs to make the reader feel as if the events were happening to him or her; it is the least-used method of narrating stories.)

   C. Third Person: A narrator who is not one of the characters tells the story. Often, this narrator is not even discussed. (*Andrew* walked into a room, but *he* did not know anyone.)
   As with many choices that an author makes, there is not one right or wrong answer. An author must choose what he or she feels is best for the writing.

Model

1. Display or distribute Sample Passage A to the students. (Note: Keep the revisions covered.) Read it aloud.

Sample Passage A

Third Person/Unknown Narrator:
Bradley went to the zoo with his friend Madeline, but before he knew it, he was all alone in a crowd of people he did not know. It was hot, and he was hungry and tired. He began to wish that they had selected something else to do.

Then, model how to revise Sample Passage A by changing the narrator using a Think-Aloud, or have the students help you make the revisions. Remind the students that Madeline also could be the narrator of this passage.

Know Your Narrator *(cont.)*

Sample Revisions

Bradley as the narrator:

I went to the zoo with my friend Madeline, but before I knew it, I was all alone in a crowd of people I did not know. It was hot, and I was hungry and tired. I began to wish that we had selected something else to do.

You as the narrator:

You went to the zoo with your friend Madeline, but before you knew it, you were all alone in a crowd of people that you did not know. It was hot, and you were hungry and tired. You began to wish that you had selected something else to do.

Madeline as the narrator:

I went to the zoo with my friend Bradley, but before I knew it, I was all alone in a crowd of people that I did not know. It was hot, and I felt alone and a little nervous. I hoped that I would find Bradley soon. (Point out that Madeline and Bradley probably will have different feelings and different perspectives on the same situation.)

Use the Tool

Apply

Remind the students that they will not always be able to use their new revision skills immediately, and they might not be able to use each of their revision tools for every piece of writing. But, they should consider each of their tools every time they revise.

Ask students to try to apply their new skill to their own writing. As students are working, walk around the room offering suggestions, monitoring understanding, and clarifying concepts. Then, ask the students to share some of their revisions.

Reinforce Previous Skills

Review and Implement

Ask the students to take out their lists of Revision Tools (overhead and handout, page 54). Instruct students to add the new skill onto their list while you do the same on your copy.

Select to tell the story in either first, second, or third person.

- *first person—one of the characters (I)*

- *second person—you*

- *third person—he/she (character's name could be inserted here)*

Think about how the story could be told differently depending on who tells it.

Then, review the other revision skills that are on the list. Give students time to revise their work, considering each revision tool that they have. (Sometimes, you might ask the students to revise in pairs or in small groups, as well as revising individually.)

Know Your Narrator *(cont.)*

Seal it Together

Reflect and Assess

1. Have students complete the Personal Reflection and Skill Check handout (page 56) to reflect upon the revision process. For guidance, students can refer to the suggested sentence starters on the Personal Reflection Guide (page 55). Or, students can create their own reflections.

2. Then, have students complete the Skill Check (overhead or handout, page 45) to assess their ability to use the new revision tool that was introduced. Students should write their answers on their Personal Reflection and Skill Check handouts.

Skill Check

Revise this passage by selecting a different narrator to tell the story.

My friend, Jeffrey, and I are trying to decide where to go for our summer vacation. Jeffrey wants to go to an amusement park because he loves roller coaster. But I think that amusement parks are crowded, hot and expensive. I'd rather go to a National Park to hike, relax and see some beautiful sights.

---

3. Collect and review the students' work. You may opt to grade the work.

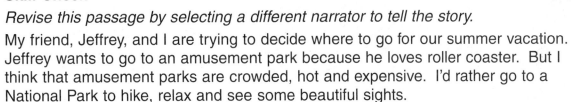

Sample Student Response

Jeffrey and Maria are trying to decide where to go for their summer vacation. Jeffrey wants to go to an amusement park because he loves roller coasters. But Maria thinks that amusement parks are crowded, hot and expensive. Maria would rather go to a National Park to hike, relax and see some beautiful sights. But Jeffrey hates National Parks! He thinks that they are buggy and boring.

Extension Ideas

- Discuss how some narrators know what is going to happen later on in the story. Those narrators can leave clues or add excitement to the writing. (Example—*If only David knew what would happen next!*)

- Discuss how some authors choose to tell a story using more than one narrator. Usually, there is a chapter break, or a line break, to help the reader realize that the narrator has changed.

Add Adjectives and Adverbs

Objective

Students will use adjectives and adverbs to enhance their writing.

Materials Needed

- Revision Tools (overhead and/or handout, page 54)

- Personal Reflection Guide (overhead, page 55)

- Lesson Five Skill Check (overhead or handout, page 76)

- Personal Reflection and Skill Check (handout, page 56)

Build a New Skill

Introduce

1. Write the following sentence on the board:

   The tree in the yard had a nest.

2. Explain that authors need to look for places to make their writing more descriptive. Descriptions help readers picture what the author is describing and makes the writing more interesting. Adding adjectives and adverbs to writing is one way to make writing more descriptive.

   An adjective is a word that describes a noun (a person, place, thing, or idea).

   An adverb is a word that answers *how?, when?, where?, in what way?, how often?, or how much?*

Model

1. Refer students back to the sentence that you wrote on the board: **The tree in the yard had a nest**. Use a Think-Aloud to model how adverbs and adjectives can be added to a sentence, or have the students help you revise the sentence.

Sample Revision

Every spring, the beautiful, huge magnolia tree in the yard had a tiny blue-jay nest right at eye-level.

Use the Tool

Apply

Remind the students that they will not always be able to use their new revision skills immediately, and they might not be able to use each of their revision tools for every piece of writing. But, they should consider each of their tools every time they revise.

Ask students to try to apply their new skill to their own writing. As students are working, walk around the room offering suggestions, monitoring understanding, and clarifying concepts. Then, ask the students to share some of their revisions.

Add Adjectives and Adverbs *(cont.)*

Reinforce Previous Skills

Review and Implement

Ask the students to take out their lists of Revision Tools (overhead and handout, page 54). Instruct students to add the new skill onto their lists while you do the same on your copy.

Add adjectives and adverbs to add details to your writing. Adjectives are words that describe people, places, things or ideas. Adverbs answer questions such as how?, when?, where?, in what way?, how often, or how much?

Then, review the other revision skills that are on the list. Give students time to revise their work, considering each revision tool that they have. (Sometimes, you might ask the students to revise in pairs or in small groups, as well as revising individually.)

Seal it Together

Reflect and Assess

1. Have students complete the Personal Reflection handout (page 56) to reflect upon the revision process. For guidance, students can refer to the suggested sentence starters on the Personal Reflection Guide (overhead or handout, page 55). Or, students can create their own reflections.

2. Then, have students complete the Skill Check to assess their ability to use the new revision tool that was introduced. Students should write their answers on their Personal Reflection and Skill Check handouts.

> **Skill Check**
> *Revise this sentence by adding adverbs and/or adjectives.*
> There were mosquitoes flying around the pond.

3. Teachers should collect and review the students' work. Teachers may opt to grade the work.

> **Sample Student Response**
> All summer long, there were billions of mosquitoes flying around the majestic pond.

Extension Ideas

This lesson attempts to encourage students to use descriptive words in their writing. You might want to spend more time examining, identifying, and using adjectives and adverbs.

Vary Sentence Length

Objective

Students will vary the length of their sentences in their writing.

Materials Needed

- Revision Tools (overhead and/or handout, page 54)
- Sample Passages A, B, and C (overhead or handout, page 61)
- Personal Reflection Guide (overhead or handout, page 55)

- Lesson Six Skill Check (overhead or handout, page 76)
- Personal Reflection and Skill Check (handout, page 56)

Build a New Skill

Introduce

1. Display and read aloud Sample Passage A or distribute your handout.

> **Sample Passage A**
>
> Sometimes, a sentence can be very long in order to give a lot of specific details, or to list many things, or to give great descriptions about something, or to tell many different events that happened, and still, that sentence is not a run-on sentence! Other sentences are just regular sentences of normal length. Wow! Some sentences can be short, too!

2. Ask: **Why might authors purposely vary the lengths of their sentences?**

   Authors vary the lengths of sentences to make their writing more interesting. Long sentences are important because they offer a lot of information, but it would be difficult to read an entire passage that consisted only of lengthy sentences. Short sentences are easy to read, but a series of short sentences can quickly become boring.

Model

1. Display and read aloud Sample Passage B and Sample Passage C to the students.

> **Sample Passage B**
>
> Yesterday, we had a cookout. It was fabulous! We had hamburgers and hot dogs. We also had salads and different toppings. Plus, we had delicious desserts. I wish that we could have cookouts like that more often.

> **Sample Passage C**
>
> Yesterday, we had a cookout. It was fabulous! We had hamburgers, hot dogs, different toppings, salads, and delicious desserts. Too bad it ended so quickly!

2. Ask: **What revisions were made to Sample Passage C?**

   Sentences 3, 4, and 5 were combined to create one longer sentence listing all of the foods that were served at the cookout. Also, the final sentence was shortened.

3. Remind students that there is more than one way that Sample Passage B could have been revised.

Vary Sentence Length *(cont.)*

Use the Tool

Apply

Remind the students that they will not always be able to use their new revision skills immediately, and they might not be able to use each of their revision tools for every piece of writing. But, they should consider each of their tools every time they revise.

Ask students to try to apply their new skill to their own writing. As students are working, walk around the room offering suggestions, monitoring understanding, and clarifying concepts. Then, ask the students to share some of their revisions.

Reinforce Previous Skills

Review and Implement

Ask the students to take out their lists of Revision Tools and Skill Check (overhead and handout, page 54). Instruct students to add the new skill onto their lists while you do the same on your copy.

Think about the lengths of your sentences. Look for places where adding longer or shorter sentences might improve your writing.

Then, review the other revision skills that are on the list. Give students time to revise their work, considering each revision tool that they have. (Sometimes, you might ask the students to revise in pairs or in small groups, as well as revising individually.)

Seal it Together

Reflect and Assess

1. Have students complete the Personal Reflection and Skill Check handout (page 56) to reflect upon the revision process. For guidance, students can refer to the suggested sentence starters on the Personal Reflection Guide (page 55). Or, students can create their own reflections.

2. Then, have students complete the Skill Check to assess their ability to use the new revision tool that was introduced. Have students write their answers on the Personal Reflection and Skill Check handouts.

Skill Check

Revise this passage by varying the length of one or more sentences in the passage provided.

There are several reasons that dogs are great companions. Dogs need to be walked. Walks keep their owners healthy. Owners can talk to their dogs. Dogs never tell secrets. Dogs don't care what owners watch on TV. As long as dogs are cuddling with their owners, they are happy.

Vary Sentence Length (cont.)

3. Collect and review the students' work. You may opt to grade the work.

Sample Student Response

Dogs are great companions. Dogs need to be walked, and walks keep their owners health. Dogs can't talk. So, owners can tell their dogs all of their secrets. Dogs are not fussy about what they watch on TV. As long as dogs are cuddling with their owners, they are happy.

Extension Ideas

- Examine some published works. See how different authors vary sentence lengths.
- While examining published authors, discuss why specific sentences are short and others are long.

Avoid Repetitions

Objective

Students will avoid repeating words.

Materials Needed

- Revision Tools (overhead and/or handout, page 54)

- Sample Passage A (overhead or handout, page 62)

- Personal Reflection Guide (overhead or handout, page 55)

- Lesson Seven Skill Check (overhead or handout, page 76)

- Personal Reflection and Skill Check (handout, page 56)

Build a New Skill

Introduce

1. Display or distribute Sample Passage A (overhead or handout, page 62). Read it aloud.

> **Sample Passage A**
>
> Some people are naturally good writers. Some people are good writers, but need a lot of help editing their work. Some people need to work hard to produce a good piece of writing.

2. Ask: **What major revision does Sample Passage A need?**

   "Some people" is used too frequently in Sample Passage A. Other words need to be used in order to avoid repeating the same words.

3. **Why do authors want to avoid repeating words?**

   Answers will vary, but should include that when words are repeated, writing can become boring.

Model

1. Use a Think-Aloud to revise Sample Passage A, or have the students help you to revise the passage.

> **Sample Revision**
>
> Some people are naturally good writers. Other people are good writers, but need a lot of help editing their work. Most people need to work hard to produce a good piece of writing.

2. Remind students that there is more than one way that Sample Passage A could have been revised. Also, remind students to look for repeated words within sentences, as well as in the beginning of sentences. (For example: We had a *fabulous* vacation this past summer. The sights were magnificent, and the food was *fabulous*.) You may also wish to discuss whether the word "good" was repeated too frequently in the passage.

Avoid Repetitions *(cont.)*

Use the Tool

Apply

Remind the students that they will not always be able to use their new revision skills immediately, and they might not be able to use each of their revision tools for every piece of writing. But, they should consider each of their tools every time they revise.

Ask students to try to apply their new skill to their own writing. As students are working, walk around the room offering suggestions, monitoring understanding, and clarifying concepts. Then, ask the students to share some of their revisions.

Reinforce Previous Skills

Review and Implement

Ask the students to take out their lists of Revision Tools (overhead and handout, page 54) Instruct students to add the new skill onto their lists while you do the same on your copy.

Avoid repeating the same word when writing, unless you have a specific reason for doing so.

Then, review the other revision skills that are on the list. Give students time to revise their work, considering each revision tool that they have. (Sometimes, you might ask the students to revise in pairs or in small groups, as well as revising individually.)

Seal it Together

Reflect and Assess

1. Have students complete the Personal Reflection and Skill Check handout (page 56) to reflect upon the revision process. For guidance, students can refer to the suggested sentence starters on the Personal Reflection Guide (page 55). Or, students can create their own reflections.

2. Then, have students complete the Skill Check to assess their ability to use the new revision tool that was introduced. Have students write their answers on their Personal Reflection and Skill Check handouts.

Skill Check

Revise this passage by replacing one or more repeated word.

This weekend was exhausting. I helped my father build a huge fence. Building the fence was a huge job. Although it was exhausting work, I feel good about having completed the huge job.

3. Collect and review the students' work. You may opt to grade the work.

Sample Student Response

This weekend was exhausting. I helped my father build a huge fence. Building the fence was a big job. Although it was hard work, I feel good about having completed the job.

Repeat to Add Rhythm

Objective
Students will strategically repeat words.

Materials Needed
- Revision Tools (overhead and/or handout, page 54)
- Sample Passages A and B (overhead or handout, page 63)
- Personal Reflection Guide (overhead, page 55)
- Lesson Eight Skill Check (overhead or handouts, page 77)
- Personal Reflection and Skill Check (handout, page 56)

Build a New Skill

Introduce
1. Explain that sometimes when words are repeated in a passage, the writing comes across as unpolished. But sometimes, authors select to repeat words, or a series of words, in order to add a rhythm to their writing, or to make a particular point. Songs and poems in particular use the method of repeating words to create a rhythm.
2. Display or distribute the Sample Passage A. Read it aloud.

> ### Sample Passage A
> The snowfall made the land look like it was covered with a white blanket. The treetops were white, the grass was white, the rooftops were white, and every car in the parking lot was white. No other color, except the brilliant blue on the blue jay, could be seen anywhere that morning.

In this passage, the author chose to repeat the color white. Ask: **Why might this author have made that decision?**

The author was trying to describe just how white the snow made everything appear, and the author was trying to show a contrast to the blue color of the bird.

Model
1. Display and read aloud Sample Passage B.

> ### Sample Passage B
> Drip! Drop! The rain kept falling. Everything was wet. The squirrels were soggy, the trees were well bathed, and the ground was saturated. Wouldn't the sun ever peer out from beneath the clouds?

2. Use a Think-Aloud as you model how to revise the passage by adding a repeated word. Or, have the students help you revise the passage.

> ### Sample Revision
> Drip! Drop! The rain kept falling. Drip! Everything was wet. Drop! The squirrels were soggy, the trees were well bathed, and the ground was saturated. Drip! Drop! Wouldn't the sun ever peer out from beneath the clouds?

Repeat to Add Rhythm *(cont.)*

Use the Tool

Apply

Remind the students that they will not always be able to use their new revision skills immediately, and they might not be able to use each of their revision tools for every piece of writing. But, they should consider each of their tools every time they revise.

Ask students to try to apply their new skill to their own writing. As students are working, walk around the room offering suggestions, monitoring understanding, and clarifying concepts. Then, ask the students to share some of their revisions.

Reinforce Previous Skills

Review and Implement

Ask the students to take out their list of Revision Tools (overhead and handout, page 54). Instruct students to add the new skill onto their list while you do the same on your copy.

Repeat a word, or a series of words, to create a rhythm, or make a particular point.

Then, review the other revision skills that are on the list. Give students time to revise their work, considering each revision tool that they have.

Seal It Together

Reflect and Assess

1. Have students complete the Personal Reflection handout (page 56) to reflect upon the revision process. For guidance, students can refer to the suggested sentence starters on the Personal Reflection Guide (page 55). Or, students can create their own reflections.

2. Then, have students complete the Skill Check to assess their ability to use the new revision tool that was introduced. Students should write their answers on their Personal Reflection and Skill Check handouts.

Skill Check ✔

Revise this sentence by repeating a word, or a series of words.

Just thinking about camping makes me itchy. There are so many bugs everywhere. Spiders crawl into the tent, mosquitoes take more bites out of me than I take of my dinner, and insects of all kinds get attracted to whatever light source I choose to use. Give me a hotel room anytime!

---

3. Collect and review the students' work. You may opt to grade the work.

Sample Student Response

Just thinking about camping drives me buggy. There are so many bugs everywhere. Bugs crawl into the tent, mosquitoes take more bites of me than I take of my dinner, and bugs of all kinds get attracted to whatever light source I choose to use. Give me a hotel room anytime!

Extension Ideas

- Locate and show students samples of published works (songs, stories, poems, etc.) where authors selected to repeat words. Discuss what effect the repetition has on the reader, or why the author might have decided to repeat those words.

Select a Format

Objective

Students will select an appropriate format for a piece of writing.

Materials Needed

- Revision Tools (overhead and/or handout, page 54)
- Activity A and B (overhead or handout, page 64)
- Personal Reflection Guide (overhead, page 55)
- Lesson Nine Skill Check (overhead or handout, page 77)
- Personal Reflection and Skill Check (handout, page 56)

Build a New Skill

Introduce

1. Define the word format for the students. A format is a way of organizing and presenting information. Explain that there are many different formats to choose from when writing.

2. Ask: **What are different formats that authors can use when they write?** (Write responses on the board. Encourage students to think about the types of writing they and their family members are asked to complete.)

   Answers will vary, but might include poetry, journals, diaries, business letters, friendly letters, paragraphs, essays, research papers, stories, plays, lists, news articles, cartoons, e-mails, directions, grants, proposals, or briefs.

3. Display or distribute Activity A. Read it aloud. Have the students select an appropriate format for each of the following situations. Answers will vary, but encourage students to explain their selections.

Activity A

Suggest an appropriate format for each of the following situations:

1. A person wants to share an experience playing an exciting basketball game.
2. A person wants to apply for a summer job.
3. A person has an idea for a great game, and wants to submit the idea to a gaming company.
4. A student needs to tell what she learned about a particular subject.
5. A person wants to share his feelings.

Sample Student Responses

1. Formats might include a story or news report.
2. Formats might include a business letter.
3. Formats might include a business letter or proposal.
4. Formats might include a paragraph, essay, or report.
5. Formats might include a journal entry, friendly letter, or poem.

Select a Format *(cont.)*

Model

1. Read aloud Activity B.

Activity B

Evaluate whether or not an appropriate format was selected.

I really want this job,

I really want this job,

I will work hard, you will see,

If you'll just hire me!

---

2. With the students, evaluate whether or not an appropriate format was selected in Activity B. *For example, although the poem shows creativity, it is not a usual format for a job request. A business letter would be a more appropriate format.*

Use the Tool

Apply

Remind the students that they will not always be able to use their new revision skills immediately, and they might not be able to use each of their revision tools for every piece of writing. But, they should consider each of their tools every time they revise.

Ask students to try to apply their new skill to their own writing. As students are working, walk around the room offering suggestions, monitoring understanding, and clarifying concepts. Then, ask the students to share some of their revisions.

Reinforce Previous Skills

Review and Implement

Ask the students to take out their lists of Revision Tools (overhead and handout, page 54). Instruct students to add the new skill onto their lists while you do the same on your copy.

Select the appropriate format for a piece of writing.

Then, review the other revision skills that are on the list. Give students time to revise their work, considering each revision tool that they have. (Sometimes, you might ask the students to revise in pairs or in small groups, as well as revising individually.)

Seal It Together

Reflect and Assess

1. Have students complete the Personal Reflection and Skill Check handout (page 56) to reflect upon the revision process. For guidance, students can refer to the suggested sentence starters on the Personal Reflection Guide (page 55). Or, students can create their own reflections.

Select a Format *(cont.)*

2. Then, have students complete the Skill Check to assess their ability to use the new revision tool that was introduced.

Skill Check

Identify appropriate written formats for the following situations:

1. You searched the internet and learned a lot about different types of frogs. Now, you need to tell your teacher what you learned.

2. You want to share a particularly funny conversation that you had with your friend.

3. You are dissatisfied with a product that you purchased, and you want a refund.

3. Collect and review the students' work. You may opt to grade the work.

Sample Student Response

1. Suggested formats might be an essay, paragraph, or research paper.

2. Suggested formats might be a story or play.

3. Suggested formats might include a business letter.

Extension Ideas

• Display samples of different writing formats.

• Show students how to find samples of different writing formats to use as a model for their own writing in grammar books, on the internet, or using other sources.

Examine the Opening

Objective

Students will use specific strategies in an attempt to capture a reader's attention.

Materials Needed

- Revision Tools (overhead and/or handout, page 54)
- Sample Passages A and B (overhead or handout, page 65)
- Personal Reflection Guide (overhead or handout, page 55)
- Lesson Ten Skill Check (overhead or hoandout, page 77)
- Personal Reflection and Skill Check (handout, page 56)

Build a New Skill

Introduce

1. Ask: **How does a writer get people interested in reading what he or she has written?**
   Answers will vary. Make sure to point out that one way writers interest readers is by creating an interesting opening.

2. Together with the students, create a list of interesting ways to begin a piece of writing. Answers will vary, but you might want to include:
   - Select an interesting piece of dialogue. ("What was that noise?")
   - Insert an exclamation. (Bam! A door slammed shut in the other room.)
   - Describe an interesting character or setting. (Johnny was an unusual fellow.)
   - Start with an exciting event. (I ran through the forest as fast as I could, trying to find a familiar sight.)
   - Appeal to the senses by describing an interesting smell, sight, sound, feel or taste. (My nose burned with the smell of smoke.)
   - Ask the reader to imagine something. (Imagine that ....)

Model

1. Display or distribute Sample Passages A and B. (Note: They are not introductory paragraphs. They are just the opening lines.)

> **Sample Passage A**
> Imagine a mossy pond with flies and mosquitoes buzzing around. Does that sound like a great vacation spot? For a frog, it is.

> **Sample Passage B**
> Frogs are interesting animals. They like to live in mossy ponds with flies and mosquitoes.

2. Ask: **Which sample passage models a more interesting way to start a writing piece about frogs?** *Sample A is the more effective opener.*

Examine the Opening *(cont.)*

Ask: **Why is Sample Passage A more interesting?** *Sample Passage A creates an image in the reader's mind. It appeals to the senses of sound and sight, and it encourages the readers to think by asking a question.*

Use the Tool

Apply

Remind the students that they will not always be able to use their new revision skills immediately, and they might not be able to use each of their revision tools for every piece of writing. But, they should consider each of their tools every time they revise.

Ask students to try to apply their new skill to their own writing. As students are working, walk around the room offering suggestions, monitoring understanding, and clarifying concepts. Then, ask the students to share some of their revisions.

Reinforce Previous Skills

Review and Implement

Ask the students to take out their list of Revision Tools (overhead and handout, page 54). Instruct students to add the new skill onto their list while you do the same on your copy.

Examine the opening to make sure that it catches the reader's attention. For example, select an interesting piece of dialogue, insert an exclamation, describe an interesting character or setting, start with an exciting event, appeal to the senses, ask the reader to imagine something, or ask a question.

Then, review the other revision skills that are on the list. Give students time to revise their work, considering each revision tool that they have. (Sometimes, you might ask the students to revise in pairs or in small groups, as well as revising individually.)

Seal it Together

Reflect and Assess

1. Have students complete the Personal Reflection and Skill Check handout (page 56) to reflect upon the revision process. For guidance, students can refer to the suggested sentence starters on the Personal Reflection Guide (page 55). Or, students can create their own reflections.

2. Then, have students complete the Skill Check to assess their ability to use the new revision tool that was introduced.

Skill Check

Rewrite this introductory sentence about springtime to make it more interesting. You may use more than one sentence to make the revision.
Springtime is a pretty time of the year.

---

3. Collect and review the students' work. You may opt to grade the work.

Sample Student Response:
Look at the rainbow of flowers on the ground! Feel the crisp, clean air! Hear the birds singing! It must be springtime.

Extension Idea

Examine how published authors begin their stories.

Be Sense-ible

Objective

Students will use descriptive language that appeals to the senses.

Materials Needed

- Revision Tools (overhead and handout, page 54)
- Sample Passages A and B (overhead or handout, page 66)

- Personal Reflection Guide (overhead or handout, page 55)
- Lesson Eleven Skill Check (overhead or handout, page 78)
- Personal Reflection and Skill Check (handout, page 56)

Build a New Skill

Introduce

1. Ask: **What are the five senses?**

   The five senses are touch, sight, smell, hearing, and taste.

   Explain that when authors are writing, they try to appeal to readers' senses. By describing the way things feel, look, smell, sound and taste, the reader can picture the scene easily and accurately.

2. Create an overhead and display or distribute Sample Passages A and B.

Sample Passage A

The sheep were grazing in a beautiful meadow.

Sample Passage B

The puffy, white sheep were grazing in the lush, green meadow. There was a light breeze blowing that carried with it the scent of fresh lavender from the hills nearby. The occasional sound of a baa could be heard. No photograph could accurately capture this scene.

---

3. Ask: **What senses does Sample Passage B describe?**

   Sample Passage B appeals to the sense of sight (puffy, white sheep), feel (Light breeze), smell (the scent of lavender), and hearing (the sound of a baa).

Model

Write the following sentence on the board: **There was so much happening at the baseball stadium.** Then, Think-Aloud or ask the students to help you revise the sentence so that sensory descriptions are included.

Sample Revision

The baseball stadium was full of people sporting their favorite team colors. Music was blaring, and the bass was pounding. The smell of hot dogs, popcorn, peanuts and cotton candy blended together. Sweat was pouring off me from the heat. There was nowhere else I'd rather have been at that moment.

Use the Tool

Apply

Remind the students that they will not always be able to use their new revision skills immediately, and they might not be able to use each of their revision tools for every piece of writing. But, they should consider each of their tools every time they revise.

Be Sense-ible *(cont.)*

Ask students to try to apply their new skill to their own writing. As students are working, walk around the room offering suggestions, monitoring understanding, and clarifying concepts. Then, ask the students to share some of their revisions.

Reinforce Previous Skills

Review and Implement

Ask the students to take out their lists of Revision Tools (overhead and handout, page 54). Instruct students to add the new skill onto their lists while you do the same on your copy.

Appeal to the reader's senses by describing what things look like, smell like, feel like, sound like, and taste like.

Then, review the other revision skills that are on the list. Give students time to revise their work, considering each revision tool that they have. (Sometimes, you might ask the students to revise in pairs or in small groups, as well as revising individually.)

Seal It Together

Reflect and Assess

1. Have students complete the Personal Reflection and Skill Check handout (page 56) to reflect upon the revision process. For guidance, students can refer to the suggested sentence starters on the Personal Reflection Guide (page 55). Or, students can create their own reflections.

2. Then, have students complete the Skill Check to assess their ability to use the new revision tool that was introduced.

Skill Check

Add three or more sensory descriptions to make this a more descriptive passage. (You might need more than one sentence to do this.)

Sam's room was a mess.

---

3. Collect and review the students' work. You may opt to grade the work.

Sample Student Response

Sam's room was a mess. Clean and dirty clothes were strewn about the room. The smell of sweaty socks permeated the air. A CD jacket lay open and broken on the floor. The alarm clocks' buzzing was muffled from underneath a pile of stuff. If I could only find the item I was looking for, I could quickly leave.

Extension Ideas

- Examine how published authors appeal to different senses in their writing.

- Have students create five columns on a piece of paper and label each column with one of each of the senses. Have some students read their descriptions aloud to the class. Have students write down the sensory descriptions that they hear in the correct columns on their papers.

Add Alliteration

Objective

Students will add alliteration to writing to create a rhythmic sound.

Materials Needed

- Revision Tools (overhead and handout, page 54)
- Personal Reflection Guide (overhead or handout, page 55)
- Lesson Twelve Skill Check (overhead or handout, page 78)
- Personal Reflection and Skill Check (handout, page 56)

Build a New Skill

Introduce

1. Write the following sentence on the board: **Playful penguins parade on the pier.**

   Ask: **What do you notice about this sentence?**

   Answers should include that the sound /p/ is repeated.

   Ask: **Why might an author wish to repeat a sound?**

   Repeating sounds is playful, and adds a rhythmic quality.

   Explain that the repetition of a sound in a piece of writing is referred to as alliteration.

Model

1. Write the following sentence on the board: **Children play on the playground equipment.**

   Then, Think-Aloud, or encourage the students to help, as you revise the sentence, adding alliteration.

Sample Revisions

Children creep and climb across the equipment.

Prancing children play on the pretty playground.

Use the Tool

Apply

Remind the students that they will not always be able to use their new revision skills immediately, and they might not be able to use each of their revision tools for every piece of writing. But, they should consider each of their tools every time they revise.

Ask students to try to apply their new skill to their own writing. As students are working, walk around the room offering suggestions, monitoring understanding, and clarifying concepts. Then, ask the students to share some of their revisions.

Reinforce Previous Skills

Review and Implement

Ask the students to take out their lists of Revision Tools (overhead and handout, page 54). Instruct students to add the new skill onto their lists while you do the same on your copy.

Add alliteration by repeating sounds to add a playful, rhythmic quality to your writing.

Add Alliteration *(cont.)*

Then, review the other revision skills that are on the list. Give students time to revise their work, considering each revision tool that they have. (Sometimes, you might ask the students to revise in pairs or in small groups, as well as revising individually.)

Seal It Together

Reflect and Assess

1. Have students complete the Personal Reflection and Skill Check handout (page 56) to reflect upon the revision process. For guidance, students can refer to the suggested sentence starters on the Personal Reflection Guide (page 55). Or, students can create their own reflections.

2. Then, have students complete the Skill Check to assess their ability to use the new revision tool that was introduced.

Skill Check
Revise this advertisement by adding alliteration to create at least one sound that is repeated three or more times.
Our Barbeque is Superb!

3. Collect and review the students' work. You may opt to grade the work.

Sample Student Responses
Our Beef Barbeque is the Best!
We Sell Barbeque that is Simply Superb!

Extension Ideas
- Locate and share advertisements that use alliteration.
- Examine poetry or other written work that uses alliteration.

Move Your Memory

Objective

Students will draw upon their own experiences to add realistic details to characters, settings, and events in their writing.

Materials Needed

- Revision Tools (overhead and handout, page 54)
- Sample Passages A, B, and C (overhead and handout, page 67)
- Personal Reflection Guide (overhead, page 55)
- Lesson Thirteen Skill Check (overhead or handout, page 78)
- Personal Reflection and Skill Check (handout, page 56)

Build a New Skill

Introduce

1. On the board, list one experience that really happened to you, and one experience that never happened to you. Have the students guess which experience is true. For example:

    A. *I went on a trip to _____.*

    B. *I performed in an opera on Broadway when I was younger.*

    Then, ask students to take out a piece of paper and write down one experience that really happened to them, and one experience that never happened to them. Allow students time to share their experiences, and have other students guess which experiences are true and which are not.

2. Point out that each student has had unique experiences in their lives. Finding these experiences, and weaving them into their writing, will make students' writing more realistic and interesting. Remind students that readers do not have to know which experiences that they've written about really happened.

3. Remind students that when thinking about experiences, students should think about people that they've met, places that they've been, and events that have occurred. These details can be used to help create believable characters, interesting settings, and realistic events.

Model

1. Display or distribute Sample Passages A, B, and C.

Sample Passages A, B, and C

A. **Character Description**

Bingo is the best dog in the world.

B. **Setting Description**

The beach was spectacular.

C. **Event Description**

After their busy day, they decided to go out for dinner. The dinner at the restaurant was horrible.

Move Your Memory *(cont.)*

2. Use a Think-Aloud as you draw upon your experiences, or ask questions and encourage students to help revise the passages. Sample questions might be:

   A. **What are some qualities that you've liked about dogs that you've seen or met?**

   B. **What beautiful beaches have you seen, either in pictures, movies or in person?**

   C. **What horrible experiences have you had at restaurants?**

Sample Revisions

A. Bingo is the best dog in the world. He is a German Shepherd who wouldn't hurt a fly. Neighborhood children run up to him so that he can give them wet, sloppy kisses. He knows some tricks, such as rolling over, and catching flying disks, but best of all, he is a great TV companion. He loves to cuddle up on the sofa while I relax and watch a movie.

B. The beach was spectacular. The sand was white as snow, and the water was clear and bluish green. Few people were there, allowing me to capture the beauty on camera without interference. I stayed until sunset, and saw the sun paint the water orange, pink, red, and gold.

C. After their busy day, they decided to go out for dinner. Dinner was horrible. First, they had to wait over an hour for a table, even though they were told that the wait would be short. Then, once they were seated, they had to wait again to get menus. When the food finally did arrive, it was cold, and some parts of the order were wrong. To top it all off, dinner was expensive!

Use the Tool

Apply

Remind the students that they will not always be able to use their new revision skills immediately, and they might not be able to use each of their revision tools for every piece of writing. But, they should consider each of their tools every time they revise.

Ask students to try to apply their new skill to their own writing. As students are working, walk around the room offering suggestions, monitoring understanding, and clarifying concepts. Then, ask the students to share some of their revisions.

Reinforce Previous Skills

Review and Implement

Ask the students to take out their lists of Revision Tools (overhead and handout, page 54). Instruct students to add the new skill onto their lists while you do the same on your copy.

Draw upon your own personal experiences to add realistic details to your writing. Think about places you've been, people you know, and events that have occurred.

Then, review the other revision skills that are on the list. Give students time to revise their work, considering each revision tool that they have. (Sometimes, you might ask the students to revise in pairs or in small groups, as well as revising individually.)

Move Your Memory *(cont.)*

Seal It Together

Reflect and Assess

1. Have students complete the Personal Reflection and Skill Check handout (page 56) to reflect upon the revision process. For guidance, students can refer to the suggested sentence starters on the Personal Reflection Guide (page 55). Or, students can create their own reflections.

2. Then, have students complete the Skill Check to assess their ability to use the new revision tool that was introduced.

> **Skill Check**
>
> *Draw upon your own experiences in order to revise this passage. You might want to think about hot days that you've experienced, different types of water you've cooled off in, or experiences you've had swimming in cold water.*
>
> It was so hot outside, and I could not wait to jump in the water. I did not realize how cold the water was until it was too late.

3. Collect and review the students' work. You may opt to grade the work.

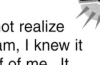

> **Sample Student Response**
>
> It was so hot outside, that could not wait to jump in the water. I did not realize how cold the water was going to be. The second my toe hit the stream, I knew it was going to be painfully cold. I could feel the heat and sweat roll off of me. It was a shock at first, but then I felt refreshed.

Extension Ideas

- Have students think about several people they know, or have seen, and have them combine those traits to create a new character.

- Have students get into groups and discuss places that they've been. Then have students use what they heard and shared to create their own setting.

- Have students think about a good, bad, and funny event that happened to them, and have them combine those events to create one new event.

Face Facts

Objective
Students will include accurate facts when writing.

Materials Needed
- Revision Tools (overhead and handout, page 54)
- Sample Passages A and B (overhead or handout, page 68)
- Personal Reflection Guide (overhead, page 55)
- Lesson Fourteen Skill Check (overhead or handout, page 79)
- Personal Reflection and Skill Check (handout, page 56)

Build a New Skill

Introduce:
1. Display Sample Passage A.

> **Sample Passage A**
> It was the year 1610. Johnny was only twelve years old, yet he had the responsibilities of a grown man. He would wake each day at 5:30 to milk the cows and feed all the animals on the farm before he drove himself to school. ✔️

   Ask: **What is wrong with Sample Passage A?**

   Answers should include that there were no cars to be driven in 1610.

2. Point out that facts need to be accurate, whether you are writing fiction or non-fiction.

   Then, ask:

   What type of non-fictional writing do you do that relies on the use of accurate facts?

   Answers might include a variety of science or historical reporting.

   What type of fictional writing would rely on accurate facts?

   Answers might include time periods or historical references (such as references to wars, famous people, etc.) within a fictional piece of writing.

   Why might an author want to include actual facts in fictional writing?

   Adding facts to fictional writing makes the writing more realistic.

   How can an author obtain facts?

   Authors can obtain facts by researching print sources, electronic sources (internet, media), or through interviews.

   Is it ever okay to alter facts?

   Only in fictional writing is it okay to alter facts, although writers should have a reason for altering facts, and then, those elements of the story become fictional. For example, science fiction writers often enhance facts to project what life might be like in the future.

Face Facts *(cont.)*

Model

1. Display and read aloud Sample Passage B.

Sample Passage B

It was the turn of the century. As New Years approached, even those people who insisted they were not worried took some precautions.

Use a Think-Aloud to add realistic facts to the passage.

Sample Revisions

It was the turn of the century. As New Years approached, even those people who insisted they were not worried took some precautions. Some people began bottling up water in case the water became contaminated. People filled up their cars in case computer systems failed and the pumps stopped working. Almost everyone withdrew at least a little extra cash…just in case.

Use the Tool

Apply

Remind the students that they will not always be able to use their new revision skills immediately, and they might not be able to use each of their revision tools for every piece of writing. But, they should consider each of their tools every time they revise.

Ask students to try to apply their new skill to their own writing. As students are working, walk around the room offering suggestions, monitoring understanding, and clarifying concepts. Then, ask the students to share some of their revisions.

Reinforce Previous Skills

Review and Implement

Ask the students to take out their lists of Revision Tools (overhead and handout, page 54). Instruct students to add the new skill onto their lists while you do the same on your copy.

Include actual facts in fictional works to make your writing more accurate; If they are not accurate, make sure that you have a reason for altering the facts. Only use accurate facts when writing non-fiction. Use print and electronic sources to gather your facts, as well as interviewing people.

Then, review the other revision skills that are on the list. Give students time to revise their work, considering each revision tool that they have. (Sometimes, you might ask the students to revise in pairs or in small groups, as well as revising individually.)

Seal It Together

Reflect and Assess

1. Have students complete the Personal Reflection and Skill Check handout (page 56) to reflect upon the revision process. For guidance, students can refer to the suggested sentence starters on the Personal Reflection Guide (page 55). Or, students can create their own reflections.

Face Facts *(cont.)*

2. Then, have students complete the Skill Check to assess their ability to use the new revision tool that was introduced. For example:

Skill Check

Add at least two accurate facts to the following passage.
That night, the President left the White House.

---

3. Collect and review the students' work. You may opt to grade the work.

Sample Student Response
That night, President Bush left the White House. He was going to talk to the American people to tell them that we were going to fight a war against terrorism.

Extension Ideas

- Take the students to the library or computer lab so that they can research accurate facts to include in their writing.

- Bring in some history books that students can search through to collect facts to include in their writing.

Tackle Transitions

Objective

Students will insert transitions in their writing.

Materials Needed

- Revision Tools (overhead and handout, page 54)
- Tackling Transitions (handout, page 69)
- Sample Passages A and B (overhead or handout, page 70)
- Personal Reflection Guide (overhead, page 55)
- Lesson Fifteen Skill Check (page 79)
- Personal Reflection and Skill Check (handout, page 56)
- Small piece of paper
- Glue

Build a New Skill

Introduce

1. Hand each student a small piece of paper. Then, assign each student a word from Tackling Transitions (handout, page 69). Students should write their assigned words on their small pieces of paper. Then, have students take turns gluing their words to a large piece of chart or bulletin board paper.

2. Explain to the students that transitions are the glue in their writing. **Transitions are the words that help connect the different ideas in their writing**. Transitions show when ideas are being added, when ideas are being contrasted, locations, movement of time, and when ideas are being concluded.

Model

1. Display or distribute Sample Passages A and B to the students. Read them aloud.

Sample Passage A

When you are feeling angry or upset, it is important to talk to someone. First of all, another person might help you to see your situation differently. Also, while trying to explain a situation to someone, you might sort out some feelings that you did not previously understand. Furthermore, just talking sometimes helps to reduce the stress. So, next time you are feeling angry or upset, be sure to find someone who you know will listen to your feelings.

Sample Passage B

Talk to someone if you are feeling angry or upset. Friends might help you to see your situation differently. Trying to explain a situation to someone, might help you sort out some feelings that you did not previously understand. Talking sometimes helps to reduce stress. If you are feeling angry or upset, be sure to find someone who you know will listen to your feelings.

Tackle Transitions *(cont.)*

2. Tell students that Sample Passage A is the better passage. Ask: **Why is Sample Passage A the better passage?**

   Answers should include that the transitions make the Sample Passage A the better passage. The transitions help connect the ideas in the passage. The transitions in the passage show when more information is being added, and when ideas are being concluded.

3. Distribute Tackling Transitions (handout, page 69). Remind students that there are many additional transitional words that can be used as well. Encourage students to keep a list of their own ideas on the backs of their handouts!

Use the Tool

Apply

Remind the students that they will not always be able to use their new revision skills immediately, and they might not be able to use each of their revision tools for every piece of writing. But, they should consider each of their tools every time they revise.

Ask students to try to apply their new skill to their own writing. As students are working, walk around the room offering suggestions, monitoring understanding, and clarifying concepts. Then, ask the students to share some of their revisions.

Reinforce Previous Skills

Review and Implement

Ask the students to take out their list of Revision Tools (overhead and handout, page 54). Instruct students to add the new skill onto their list while you do the same on your copy.

Use transitions to help connect your ideas, show differences, show locations, show amounts, show movement or time, and to when concluding ideas. (See Tackling Transitions handout.)

Then, review the other revision skills that are on the list. Give students time to revise their work, considering each revision tool that they have. (Sometimes, you might ask the students to revise in pairs or in small groups, as well as revising individually.)

Seal it Together

Reflect and Assess

1. Have students complete the Personal Reflection and Skill Check handout (page 56) to reflect upon the revision process. For guidance, students can refer to the suggested sentence starters on the Personal Reflection Guide (page 55). Or, students can create their own reflections.

Tackle Transitions *(cont.)*

2. Then, have students complete the Skill Check to assess their ability to use the new revision tool that was introduced.

Skill Check

Add at least three transitions to the following passage. Use Tackling Transitions (handout) as a reference.

It is important for children to have responsibilities. Children need to learn how to complete different types of tasks. They need to learn that sharing responsibilities makes other people's lives easier. They need to understand that their skills are needed. They need to understand that everyone does things that they might not want to do. Children do need to have responsibilities.

---

3. Collect and review the students' work. You may opt to grade the work.

Sample Student Response

It is important for children to have responsibilities. Children need to learn how to complete different types of tasks. In addition, they need to learn that sharing responsibilities makes other people's lives easier. Furthermore, they need to understand that their skills are needed, too. Lastly, they need to understand that everyone does things that they might not want to do. Therefore, children do need to have responsibilities.

Extension Ideas

- Examine published works to locate different transitions. Add new ones to the students' lists of transitions.

- Locate transitions that students naturally have already placed in their writing.

Shake Up Sentences

Objective

Students will change sentence structures to add variety to their writing.

Materials Needed

- Revision Tools (overhead and handout, page 54)
- Sample Passages A, B, and C (overhead or handout, page 71)

- Personal Reflection Guide (overhead, page 55)
- Lesson Sixteen Skill Check (overhead or handout, page 79)
- Personal Reflection and Skill Check (handout, page 56)

Build a New Skill

Introduce

1. Create an overhead and display or distribute Sample Passages A, B, and C. Read Sample Passages A, B aloud.

> ### Sample Passage A
> The ice cream truck was clanging in the distance. The children began reaching into their pockets to gather their loose change. A line began to form in the usual spot. The children could not wait for the ice cream truck to arrive.

> ### Sample Passage B
> Clanging in the distance was the ice cream truck. Reaching into their pockets, children began to gather their loose change. Forming in the usual spot was a line. The children could not wait for the ice cream truck to arrive.

2. Ask: **What is the difference between the two sample passages?**

   Answers should include that the sentences are formed differently. In Sample Passage B, the subject does not start the sentence. Instead, many of the sentences in this passage start with "ing verbs."

3. Then, read Sample Passage C aloud.

> ### Sample Passage C
> Clanging in the distance was the ice cream truck. The children began reaching into their pockets to gather their loose change. Forming in the usual spot was a line. The children could not wait for the ice cream truck to arrive.

4. Ask: **How does Sample Passage C differ from the other passages that we examined?**

   Answers should include that Sample Passage C combines the techniques of the two previous sample passages. Some sentences begin with the subject, and some begin with "ing verbs."

   Explain that varying the way sentences are formed adds interest to your writing.

Model

1. Write the following sentence on the board. **The homeless man slept on the pavement, surrounded by everything he owned.** Then, use a Think-Aloud to model how to revise this sentence by moving the subject away from the beginning of the sentence. Or, encourage the students to offer suggestions about how this sentence could be revised.

Shake Up Sentences (cont.)

Sample Revisions

Surrounded by everything he owned, the homeless man slept on the pavement.

Sleeping on the pavement, the homeless man kept warm by surrounding himself with everything that he owned.

Use the Tool

Apply

Remind the students that they will not always be able to use their new revision skills immediately, and they might not be able to use each of their revision tools for every piece of writing. But, they should consider each of their tools every time they revise.

Ask students to try to apply their new skill to their own writing. As students are working, walk around the room offering suggestions, monitoring understanding, and clarifying concepts. Then, ask the students to share some of their revisions.

Reinforce Previous Skills

Review and Implement

Ask the students to take out their lists of Revision Tools (overhead and handout, page 54). Instruct students to add the new skill onto their lists while you do the same on your copy.

Varying the way sentences are formed adds interest to your writing. Try moving the subject away from the beginning of the sentence.

Then, review the other revision skills that are on the list. Give students time to revise their work, considering each revision tool that they have.

Seal It Together

Reflect and Assess

1. Have students complete the Personal Reflection and Skill Check handout (page 56) to reflect upon the revision process. For guidance, students can refer to the suggested sentence starters on the Personal Reflection Guide (page 55). Or, students can create their own reflections.

2. Then, have students complete the Skill Check to assess their ability to use the new revision tool that was introduced.

Skill Check

Revise this sentence by moving the subject away from the beginning of the sentence. The subject of the sentence is underlined.

The <u>cat</u> was meowing loudly because it was hungry for its food.

---

3. Collect and review the students' work. You may opt to grade the work.

Sample Student Responses

Meowing loudly, the cat let me know that it was hungry for its food.

Hungry for its food, the cat was meowing loudly.

Extension Idea

- Take this opportunity for a grammar lesson. Identify subjects of sentences.

Tuning the Tone

Objective

Students will be able to create a consistent tone within a piece of writing.

Materials Needed

- Revision Tools (overhead and handout, page 54)
- Model Word Web (overhead, page 72)
- Sample Passages A and B (overhead or handout, page 73)

- Personal Reflection Guide (overhead, page 55)
- Lesson Seventeen Skill Check (overhead or handout, page 80)
- Personal Reflection and Skill Check (handout, page 56)

Build a New Skill

Introduce

1. Introduce the word *tone* to your students. **Tone is the general effect that a piece of writing has on a reader.** Tell students that *they* create the tone in their writing.

2. Have the students think about what they have written, and have them identify the tone that they want to express.

3. Then, have students create a word web to help them generate words that will help them express their intended tone. To create a word web, have the students write their intended tone in the center of a web, and then have them identify words that would describe or support that tone. Display the Model Word Web for the student, using *scary* as your tone.

Tuning the Tone *(cont.)*

Model

1. Display or distribute and Sample Passages A and B to the students. Read them aloud.

> ### Sample Passage A
> I went to the dentist's office and had a tooth filled for the first time. There was a lot of odd looking equipment at the dentists' office, and I did not like the noises that I heard, either.

> ### Sample Passage B
> My heart beat faster as we drove through the mist to get to the dentist's office. I was going to get a tooth filled for the first time, and it was a nail-biting experience. I could feel the sweat pouring off of my face as I began to examine the odd looking equipment in the office, and I did not like the dark shadows that the equipment created on the ceiling, either. Suddenly, I heard the floor begin to creak as the dentist made his way to my room.

2. Discuss with the students how Sample Passage B does a better job at creating a scary tone. (You might want to have the students pick out the words that were used to help create the tone within the writing sample. For example, mist, nail-biting, sweat, dark shadows, and creak were all used to help create the tone.)

Use the Tool

Apply

Remind the students that they will not always be able to use their new revision skills immediately, and they might not be able to use each of their revision tools for every piece of writing. But, they should consider each of their tools every time they revise.

Ask students to try to apply their new skill to their own writing. As students are working, walk around the room offering suggestions, monitoring understanding, and clarifying concepts. Then, ask the students to share some of their revisions.

Reinforce Previous Skills

Review and Implement

Ask the students to take out their lists of Revision Tools (overhead and handout, page 54). Instruct students to add the new skill onto their lists while you do the same on your copy.

Express a specific tone within a piece of writing by using words that describe or support that tone. (Tone is the general effect that a piece of writing has on a reader.)

Then, review the other revision skills that are on the list. Give students time to revise their work, considering each revision tool that they have. (Sometimes, you might ask the students to revise in pairs or in small groups, as well as revising individually.)

Tuning the Tone *(cont.)*

Seal it Together

Reflect and Assess

1. Have students complete the Personal Reflection and Skill Check handout (page 56) to reflect upon the revision process. For guidance, students can refer to the suggested sentence starters on the Personal Reflection Guide (page 55). Or, students can create their own reflections.

2. Then, have students complete the Skill Check to assess their ability to use the new revision tool that was introduced. For example:

Skill Check

Revise this passage by giving it a specific tone. To do this, identify the tone you want to create, and identify words that help describe and support the tone. Then, rewrite the passage using those words.

"The house had white paint and black shutters. The inside was empty. There was a garden in the backyard."

---

3. Collect and review the students' work. You may opt to grade the work.

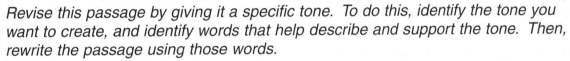

Sample Student Response

The old house had peeling white paint and black shutters that were falling off of their hinges. The inside was empty, with dust covering the floors and spider webs covering the ceilings. There was a garden in the backyard that was overgrown as well. (Tone: shabby; Support Words: old, peeling paint, dust, creaking, spider webs, overgrown, falling off.)

Extension Idea

• Read parts of students' writing, or have individual students read their own aloud. Have the rest of the class write down words that they feel help create a tone as they listen to the reading. Then, have students discuss the author's intended tone.

First Impressions (Selecting a Title)

Objective

Students will use specific techniques to select an appropriate title for a piece of writing.

Materials Needed

- Revision Tools (overhead and/or handout, page 54)
- Sample Passages A, B, and C (overhead or handout, page 74)
- Personal Reflection Guide (overhead or handout, page 55)
- Lesson Eighteen Skill Check (overhead or handout, page 80)
- Personal Reflection and Skill Check (Handout, page 56)

Build a New Skill

Introduce

1. Ask: **What are some of the first things that you see when you pick up a book, magazine, or any piece of writing?**

   Answers will vary, but should include that one of the first things you see when you pick up a piece of writing is the title.

   Ask: **What is the purpose of giving something a title?**

   Answers might vary, but should include that titles try to interest readers, give general information about the writing, and/or uniquely distinguish the writing from other pieces of writing.

   Ask: **How do you select titles for pieces of writing?**

   List responses on the board. Have students volunteer methods that they use to select titles for their writing. *Answers might include thinking about the general topic of the writing, thinking about the characters or setting, selecting an unusual or interesting phrase that is included in the writing, selecting an important concept of the writing to use as the title, or using alliteration (repetition of sounds) to come up with an interesting title.*

   Ask: **What must an author consider when selecting a title?**

   Answers might include that the author should consider the purpose of the writing (an informative piece of writing should have an informative title, a more creative piece of writing can have a more creative title), and the originality of the title.

Model

1. Display or distribute Sample Passages A, B, and C. Read the three sample passages aloud to the students.

Sample Passage A

It is important to take care of your teeth. Choose a toothbrush with soft bristles, and brush in a circular motion along your gum line. Brushing twice a day is recommended. Brushing your teeth seems obvious, but many people forget to brush their tongues. This is important to do in order to avoid plaque build-up there. Don't forget to floss, too! Flossing should be done at least once a day. Talk to your dentist to make sure that you are brushing and flossing correctly.

First Impressions *(cont.)*

Sample Passage B

Who cares about losing a tooth? You have more if one gets a hole or falls out! Toothpaste is expensive, and dental floss cuts into your fingers and hurts them! Furthermore, who has time to brush twice a day, while staring drearily into the mirror? And spitting into the sink? Yuck! That spit leaves rings in the sink, and then you need to spend time cleaning out your sink. Just pop in a piece of gum and be done!

Sample Passage C

Chomp, chomp, chomp,

Chew, chew, chew.

There are so many things your teeth can do.

Smile for the camera,

Hiss at your friend,

Be creative, there is no end.

So, take care of your teeth

Everyday

Or you may lose those teeth someday.

2. Then present these three titles to the students: *The Bother of Brushing, Chomp, Take Care of Your Teeth.*

3. Place students in small groups and ask: **Which title best fits which passage and why? What techniques were used to select the titles?** Or, use a Think-Aloud to answer these questions for the students.

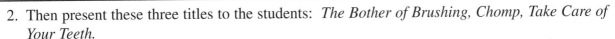

Sample Responses

"The Bother of Brushing" best fits Sample Passage B since that passage focuses on how brushing teeth is a bother. It is also humorous, like the passage. The author used alliteration to try to create an interesting sounding title.

"Chomp" best fits Sample Passage C because that is how the poem begins. The author selected a word from the passage to try to create an interesting title.

"Take Care of Your Teeth" best fits Sample Passage A because the title informs the reader about the content of the passage. The author selected the general idea of the passage to use as the title.

Use the Tool

Apply

Remind the students that they will not always be able to use their new revision skills immediately, and they might not be able to use each of their revision tools for every piece of writing. But, they should consider each of their tools every time they revise.

Ask students to try to apply their new skill to their own writing. As students are working, walk around the room offering suggestions, monitoring understanding, and clarifying concepts. Then, ask the students to share some of their revisions.

First Impressions *(cont.)*

Reinforce Previous Skills

Review and Implement

Ask the students to take out their lists of Revision Tools (overhead and handout, page 54). Instruct students to add the new skill onto their lists while you do the same on your copy.

Select a title that interests the reader, is unique, and/or is informative. Think about the general topic of the writing, the characters or setting, an unusual or interesting phrase, alliteration, or an important concept to use as the title.

Then, review the other revision skills that are on the list. Give students time to revise their work, considering each revision tool that they have. (Sometimes, you might ask the students to revise in pairs or in small groups, as well as revising individually.)

Seal it Together

Reflect and Assess

1. Have students complete the Personal Reflection and Skill Check handout (page 56) to reflect upon the revision process. For guidance, students can refer to the suggested sentence starters on the Personal Reflection Guide (page 55). Or, students can create their own reflections.

2. Then, have students complete the Skill Check to assess their ability to use the new revision tool that was introduced.

Skill Check

Select a title for the passage below. Then, answer one of the following questions:
What technique did you use to help you select the title?
Why is the title you selected effective?

My dog's favorite activity is to go swimming in a lake. She loves it when I throw sticks in for her to chase. She swims out to the stick, grabs it, and brings back to me. The only problem is, after she drops the stick in front of me, she shakes her wet fur and gets me all wet. Next time, I'm bringing an umbrella.

---

3. Collect and review the students' work. You may opt to grade the work.

Sample Student Response

A good title for the passage might be "Bring an Umbrella." A technique I used to select this title was to look for interesting words in the passage that I could use to create an interesting title.

Extension Ideas

- List titles of stories that you have read as a class this year. Have students examine why those titles might have been selected.

- Share published titles with students. Have students discuss what information the titles give the reader.

Close with a Clincher

Objective

Students will use specific techniques to bring their writing to a close.

Materials Needed

- Revision Tools (overhead and/or handout, page 54)

- Personal Reflection Guide (overhead or handout, page 55)

- Lesson Nineteen Skill Check (overhead or handout, page 80)

- Personal Reflection and Skill Check (handout, page 56)

Build a New Skill

Introduce

1. Explain that just like it is important to begin a writing passage in an interesting manner, it is also important to end a writing passage in an interesting manner.

   Ask: **Why might the ending of a writing passage be so important?**

   Answers should include that it lets the reader know the passage is over, it is the author's last chance to make a point, and it is the last thing that the reader remembers about the writing passage.

   Ask: **What techniques can an author use when trying to end a writing piece?** List answers on the board or overhead.

   Answers should include: When deciding how to end a piece of writing, an author might review the main points of the writing, ask questions to keep readers thinking, resolve problems (or select to leave problems unresolved), create space for readers to continue to imagine, and/or use transitions.

Model

1. Ask students to imagine that you just wrote a persuasive paper to the school board trying to convince them to delay the start of the day. Use a Think-Aloud to model how you might choose to end this piece of writing.

Sample Think-Aloud:

Well, if I were writing a persuasive paper to a school board, then it would be a formal piece of writing. I would need to include a formal summary paragraph. I might begin the final paragraph by selecting a transition that would let the reader know I was beginning my conclusion, and then I would try to restate my main arguments. My paragraph might sound something like this:

"In conclusion, it would be a very wise decision for you to delay the start of the school day. Students will get more sleep, and be more alert in class as a result. When students are alert, they learn more effectively. Finally, if the school day starts later, then it ends later, too. That would mean that students won't have as much unsupervised time in the afternoons, which is important to many parents. So, please, make the right choice, and delay the start of the school day."

Close with a Clincher *(cont.)*

Use the Tool

Apply

Remind the students that they will not always be able to use their new revision skills immediately, and they might not be able to use each of their revision tools for every piece of writing. But, they should consider each of their tools every time they revise.

Ask students to try to apply their new skill to their own writing. As students are working, walk around the room offering suggestions, monitoring understanding, and clarifying concepts. Then, ask the students to share some of their revisions.

Reinforce Previous Skills

Review and Implement

Ask the students to take out their lists of Revision Tools (Overhead and Handout, page 54). Instruct students to add the new skill onto their lists while you do the same on your copy.

Make sure your ending is interesting. Try to review the main points of the writing, ask questions to keep your readers thinking, resolve problems (or select to leave problems unresolved), create space for readers to continue to imagine, and/or use transitions to let the reader know you are concluding your writing.

Then, review the other revision skills that are on the list. Give students time to revise their work, considering each revision tool that they have. (Sometimes, you might ask the students to revise in pairs or in small groups, as well as revising individually.)

Seal it Together

Reflect and Assess

1. Have students complete the Personal Reflection and Skill Check handout (page 56) to reflect upon the revision process. For guidance, students can refer to the suggested sentence starters on the Personal Reflection Guide (page 55). Or, students can create their own reflections.

2. Then, have students complete the Skill Check to assess their ability to use the new revision tool that was introduced.

Skill Check

Describe a piece of writing you are currently working on, or recently completed. Select one of the following questions to answer: How did you (or could you) choose to end the writing piece? What techniques did you (or could you) use to help create the ending to your piece of writing?

Close with a Clincher *(cont.)*

3. Collect and review the students' work. You may opt to grade the work.

Sample Student Response

I am writing a creative paper about butterflies. I could end the writing by asking the readers some questions about how their lives might be different if they were butterflies in order to keep the readers thinking about butterflies.

Extension Ideas

- Locate a variety of works with different endings. Place students in small groups, and assign each group one ending to examine. Have the group decide what technique the author used to end the writing. You can continue to extend the activity by having the students create a new ending to the story.

Revision Tools

As you learn new skills to use as you revise your writing, list the skills here. Use this sheet to remind you of all the tools you have gained as you revise any of your writing. Remember, you might not be able to use each of your revision tools for every piece of writing, but you should consider each of your tools every time you revise.

_____

_____

_____

_____

_____

_____

_____

_____

_____

_____

_____

_____

_____

_____

Personal Reflection Guide

A revision skill I found particularly helpful was …_____

_____

Something new I tried today was… _____

_____

Something I did that really improved my writing was… _____

_____

Something I tried that did not work for this writing was… _____

_____

A skill I still don't understand is…_____

_____

A revision tool that I had already used in my writing was…_____

_____

Revising is important because… _____

_____

Someone helped me revise when…_____

_____

I helped someone else revise when… _____

_____

Revising helps my writing because… _____

_____

Revising helped this piece of writing because… _____

_____

I was disappointed with my revisions because… _____

_____

I had a difficult time revising because…_____

_____

Other…. _____

_____

Personal Reflection and Skill Check

Name: _____

Date: _____

Writing Piece: _____

Personal Reflection

Directions: Reflect on the revision process that you used today.

_____

_____

_____

_____

_____

Skill Check

Directions: Show your teacher that you understand the new skill that was just presented. Follow the directions provided by your teacher, and place your answer here.

_____

_____

_____

_____

_____

_____

_____

_____

Say "Said" Sixty Ways

Sample Passage A

"What do you want to do today?" said Sam.

"I don't know. Maybe we can go rollerblading in the park," said Ceil.

"I hate rollerblading," said Sam.

"Okay, so what do you want today?" said Ceil.

Sample Passage B

"What do you want to do today?" asked Sam.

"I don't know. Maybe we can go rollerblading in the park," suggested Ceil.

"I hate rollerblading," muttered Sam.

"Okay, so what do you want to do today?" retorted Ceil.

Why is it more effective to use a variety of words instead of using the word *said*?

_____

_____

_____

_____

_____

Say "Said" Sixty Ways *(cont.)*

wondered	bothered	quibbled
thought	fretted	bickered
mouthed	fussed	squabbled
whispered	mimicked	retorted
muttered	teased	disputed
murmured	joked	debated
evaded	jested	opposed
remarked	struggled	sputtered
mentioned	suggested	reacted
stated	speculated	spat
uttered	guessed	argued
spoke	asked	quarreled
bade	requested	lashed
voiced	queried	yelled
explained	answered	shouted
accounted	responded	screamed
decided	replied	exploded
determined	chimed	screeched
chose	applauded	whined
concocted	approved	mused
worried	decreed	

Vary Ways of Writing Dialogue

Sample Passage A

"What's going on here?" asked John's mother.

"We were trying to bake a cake, but the cat knocked over the cake mixture," responded John's friend, Sam.

"Where is the cat now?" wondered John's mom, aloud.

"Oh, the cat is fine! He is outside licking his paws and having a snack at the same time," laughed Sam.

Sample Passage B

John's mother asked, "What's going on here?"

"We were trying to bake a cake," responded John's friend, Sam, "but the cat knocked over the cake mixture."

"Where is the cat now?" wondered John's mom, aloud.
Sam laughed. "Oh, the cat is fine! He is outside licking his paws and having a snack at the same time."

What is the difference between the two sample passages?

_____

_____

_____

_____

_____

Why might an author choose to vary the place where the speaker is identified?

_____

_____

_____

_____

_____

Know Your Narrator

Sample Passage A

Third Person/Unknown Narrator:

Bradley went to the zoo with his friend Madeline, but before he knew it, he was all alone in a crowd of people he did not know. It was hot, and he was hungry and tired. He began to wish that they had selected something else to do.

Sample Revisions

Bradley as the narrator:

I went to the zoo with my friend Madeline, but before I knew it, I was all alone in a crowd of people I did not know. It was hot, and I was hungry and tired. I began to wish that we had selected something else to do.

You as the narrator:

You went to the zoo with your friend Madeline, but before you knew it, you were all alone in a crowd of people that you did not know. It was hot, and you were hungry and tired. You began to wish that you had selected something else to do.

Madeline as the narrator:

I went to the zoo with my friend Bradley, but before I knew it, I was all alone in a crowd of people that I did not know. It was hot, and I felt alone and a little nervous. I hoped that I would find Bradley soon. (Point out that Madeline and Bradley probably will have different feelings and different perspectives on the same situation.)

Vary Sentence Length

Sample Passage A

Sometimes, a sentence can be very long in order to give a lot of specific details, or to list many things, or to give great descriptions about something, or to tell many different events that happened, and still, that sentence is not a run-on sentence! Other sentences are just regular sentences of normal length. Wow! Some sentences can be short, too!

Why might authors purposely vary the lengths of their sentences?

_____

_____

Sample Passage B

Yesterday, we had a cookout. It was fabulous! We had hamburgers and hot dogs. We also had salads and different toppings. Plus, we had delicious desserts. I wish that we could have cookouts like that more often.

Sample Passage C

Yesterday, we had a cookout. It was fabulous! We had hamburgers, hot dogs, different toppings, salads, and delicious desserts. Too bad it ended so quickly!

What revisions were made to Sample Passage C?

_____

_____

_____

Avoid Repetitions

Sample Passage A

Some people are naturally good writers. Some people are good writers, but need a lot of help editing their work. Some people need to work hard to produce a good piece of writing.

What major revision does Sample Passage A need?

_____

_____

_____

_____

Why do authors want to avoid repeating words?

_____

_____

_____

_____

Repeat to Add Rhythm

Sample Passage A

The snowfall made the land look like it was covered with a white blanket. The treetops were white, the grass was white, the rooftops were white, and every car in the parking lot was white. No other color, except the brilliant blue on the blue jay, could be seen anywhere that morning.

In Sample Passage A, the author chose to repeat the color white. Why might this author have made that decision?

_____

_____

_____

_____

Sample Passage B

Drip! Drop! The rain kept falling. Everything was wet. The squirrels were soggy, the trees were well bathed, and the ground was saturated. Wouldn't the sun ever peer out from beneath the clouds?

How can Sample Passage B be revised?

_____

_____

_____

_____

Select a Format

Activity A

Suggest an appropriate format for each of the following situations:

1. A person wants to share an experience playing an exciting basketball game. _____

   _____

2. A person wants to apply for a summer job.

   _____

   _____

3. A person has an idea for a great game, and wants to submit the idea to a gaming company.

   _____

   _____

4. A student needs to tell what she learned about a particular subject.

   _____

   _____

5. A person wants to share his feelings.

   _____

   _____

Activity B

Evaluate whether or not an appropriate format was used for this writing selection.

I really want this job,

I really want this job,

I will work hard, you will see,

If you'll just hire me!

_____

_____

_____

_____

Examine the Opening

Sample Passage A
Imagine a mossy pond with flies and mosquitoes buzzing around. Does that sound like a great vacation spot? For a frog, it is.

Sample Passage B
Frogs are interesting animals. They like to live in mossy ponds with flies and mosquitoes. They eat flies and mosquitoes.

Which sample passage models a more interesting way to start a writing piece about frogs? Why?

_____

_____

_____

_____

_____

Be Sense-ible

Sample Passage A
The sheep were grazing in a beautiful meadow.

Sample Passage B
The puffy, white sheep were grazing in the lush, green meadow. There was a light breeze blowing that carried with it the scent of fresh lavender from the hills nearby. The occasional sound of a baa could be heard. No photograph could accurately capture this scene.

What senses does Sample Passage B appeal to?

_____

_____

_____

_____

Move Your Memory

Revise the following sample passages, drawing upon personal experiences:

Sample Passage A

Character Description

Bingo is the best dog in the world.

Sample Passage B

Setting Description

The beach was spectacular.

Sample Passage C

Event Description

After their busy day, they decided to go out for dinner. The dinner at the restaurant was horrible.

A. What are some qualities that you've liked about dogs that you've seen or met?

_____

_____

_____

_____

B. What beautiful beaches have you seen, either in pictures, movies or in person?

_____

_____

_____

_____

C. What horrible experiences have you had at restaurants?

_____

_____

_____

_____

Face Facts

Sample Passage A

It was the year 1610. Johnny was only twelve years old, yet he had the responsibilities of a grown man. He would wake each day at 5:30 to milk the cows and feed all the animals on the farm before he drove himself to school.

What is wrong with Sample Passage A?

_____

_____

What type of non-fictional writing do you do that relies on the use of accurate facts?_____

_____

_____

What type of fictional writing would rely on accurate facts?

_____

_____

Why might an author want to include actual facts in fictional writing?

_____

_____

How can an author obtain facts?

_____

_____

Is it ever okay to alter facts?

_____

_____

Sample Passage B

It was the turn of the century. As New Years approached, even those people who insisted they were not worried took some precautions.

Revise Sample Passage B by adding realistic facts.

_____

_____

_____

Tackling Transitions

When adding information, try:

additionally	another	for instance	lastly
again	as	further	likewise
also	besides	furthermore	moreover
and	finally	in addition	similarly
and then	first, secondly, etc.	in fact	the following
an example	for another	last	too

When showing differences, try:

although	even though	instead	otherwise
at the same time	however	nevertheless	still
but	in any event	on the contrary	yet
despite this	in contrast	on the other hand	

To show location, try:

above	beside	inside	onto
across	between	into	opposite to
against	beyond	in front	out
along	by	nearby	over
around	down	nearer	there
behind	down under	on	through
below	here	on the opposite side	under
beneath	in	on the other side	

When showing amount, try:

few	less than	most	several
fewer than	many	over	smaller
greater	more than	under	some

To show movement of time, try:

after	during	in the past	then
afterward	first	later	until
at last	finally	meanwhile	while
at length	immediately	not long after	
before	in a little while	suddenly	
between	in the meantime	soon	

When summarizing, try:

accordingly	for this reason	lastly	therefore
as a result	in closing	most importantly	to conclude
because	in other words	so	
consequently	in summary	then	

Tackle Transitions *(cont.)*

Sample Passage A

When you are feeling angry or upset, it is important to talk to someone. First of all, another person might help you to see your situation differently. Also, while trying to explain a situation to someone, you might sort out some feelings that you did not previously understand. Furthermore, just talking sometimes helps to reduce the stress. So, next time you are feeling angry or upset, be sure to find someone who you know will listen to your feelings.

Sample Passage B

Talk to someone if you are feeling angry or upset. Friends might help you to see your situation differently. Trying to explain a situation to someone, might help you sort out some feelings that you did not previously understand. Talking sometimes helps to reduce stress. If you are feeling angry or upset, be sure to find someone who you know will listen to your feelings.

Why is Sample Passage A the better passage?

_____

_____

_____

_____

Shake Up Sentences

Sample Passage A

The ice cream truck was clanging in the distance. The children began reaching into their pockets to gather their loose change. A line began to form in the usual spot. The children could not wait for the ice cream truck to arrive.

Sample Passage B

Clanging in the distance was the ice cream truck. Reaching into their pockets, children began to gather their loose change. Forming in the usual spot was a line. The children could not wait for the ice cream truck to arrive.

What is the difference between the two sample passages?

_____

_____

_____

_____

_____

Sample Passage C

Clanging in the distance was the ice cream truck. The children began reaching into their pockets to gather their loose change. Forming in the usual spot was a line. The children could not wait for the ice cream truck to arrive.

How does Sample Passage C differ from the other passages that we examined?

_____

_____

_____

_____

Tuning the Tone
Model Word Web

Tuning the Tone *(cont.)*

Sample Passage A

I went to the dentist's office and had a tooth filled for the first time. There was a lot of odd looking equipment at the dentists' office, and I did not like the noises that I heard, either.

Sample Passage B

My heart beat faster as we drove through the mist to get to the dentist's office. I was going to get a tooth filled for the first time, and it was a nail-biting experience. I could feel the sweat pouring off of my face as I began to examine the odd looking equipment in the office, and I did not like the dark shadows that the equipment created on the ceiling, either. Suddenly, I heard the floor begin to creak as the dentist made his way to my room.

How does Sample Passage B create a scarier tone?

_____

_____

_____

_____

_____

_____

_____

_____

First Impressions (Selecting a Title)

Sample Passage A

It is important to take care of your teeth. Choose a toothbrush with soft bristles, and brush in a circular motion along your gum line. Brushing twice a day is recommended. Brushing your teeth seems obvious, but many people forget to brush their tongues. This is important to do in order to avoid plaque build-up there. Don't forget to floss, too! Flossing should be done at least once a day. Talk to your dentist to make sure that you are brushing and flossing correctly.

Sample Passage B

Who cares about losing a tooth? You have more if one gets a hole or falls out! Toothpaste is expensive, and dental floss cuts into your fingers and hurts them! Furthermore, who has time to brush twice a day, while you staring drearily into the mirror? And spitting in to the sink? Yuck! That spit leaves rings in the sink, and then you need to spend time cleaning out your sink. Just pop in a piece of gum and be done!

Sample Passage C

Chomp, chomp, chomp,
Chew, chew, chew.
There are so many things your teeth can do.
Smile for the camera,
Hiss at your friend,
Be creative, there is no end.
So, take care of your teeth
Everyday
Or you may loose those teeth someday.

Which title best fits which passage and why?

The Bother of Brushing _____

Chomp _____

Take Care of Your Teeth _____

What techniques were used to select the titles?

_____

_____

_____

_____

Skill Checks

Lesson One—(No Skill Check)

Lesson Two

Skill Check

Revise this passage by replacing the word "said" with more descriptive words.

"It's really raining outside," said Anna.
"I know. I was planning on going outside," said Charlotte.
"Maybe we can find something interesting to do inside instead," said Anna.

Lesson Three

Skill Check

Revise this sentence by placing the speaker in another location.

"I wonder what the weather will be like this weekend," mused the child.

Lesson Four

Skill Check

Revise this passage by selecting a different narrator to tell the story.

My friend, Jeffrey, and I are trying to decide where to go for our summer vacation. Jeffrey wants to go to an amusement park because he loves roller coasters. But I think that amusement parks are crowded, hot, and expensive. I'd rather go to a National Park to hike, relax, and see some beautiful sights.

Skill Checks *(cont.)*

Lesson Five

Skill Check

Revise this sentence by adding adverbs and/or adjectives.

There were mosquitoes flying around the pond.

Lesson Six

Skill Check

Revise this passage by varying the length of one or more sentences.

There are several reasons that dogs are great companions. Dogs need to be walked. Walks keep their owners healthy. Owners can talk to their dogs. Dogs never tell secrets. Dogs don't care what owners watch on TV. As long as dogs are cuddling with their owners, they are happy.

Lesson Seven

Skill Check

Revise this passage by replacing one or more repeated words.

This weekend was exhausting. I helped my father build a huge fence. Building the fence was a huge job. Although it was exhausting work, I feel good about having completed the huge job.

Skill Checks (cont.)

Lesson Eight

Skill Check

Revise this sentence by repeating a word, or a series of words.

Just thinking about camping makes me itchy. There are so many bugs everywhere. Spiders crawl into the tent, mosquitoes take more bites out of me than I take of my dinner, and insects of all kinds get attracted to whatever light source I choose to use. Give me a hotel room anytime!

Lesson Nine

Skill Check

Identify appropriate written formats for the following situations:

1. You searched the internet and learned a lot about different types of frogs. Now, you need to tell your teacher what you learned.
2. You want to share a particularly funny conversation that you had with your friend.
3. You are dissatisfied with a product that you purchased, and you want a refund.

Lesson Ten

Skill Check

Rewrite this introductory sentence about springtime to make it more interesting. You may use more than one sentence to make the revision.

Springtime is a pretty time of the year.

Skill Checks (cont.)

Lesson Eleven

Skill Check

Add three or more sensory descriptions to make this a more descriptive passage. (You might need more than one sentence to this.)

Sam's room was a mess.

Lesson Twelve

Skill Check

Revise this advertisement by adding alliteration to create at least one sound that is repeated three or more times.

Our Barbeque is Superb!

Lesson Thirteen

Skill Check

Draw upon your own experiences in order to revise this passage. You might want to think about hot days that you've experienced, different types of water you've cooled off in, or experiences you've had swimming in cold water.

It was so hot outside that I could not wait to jump in the water. I did not realize how cold the water was until it was too late.

Skill Checks *(cont.)*

Lesson Fourteen

Skill Check

Add at least two accurate facts to the following passage.

That night, the President left the White House.

Lesson Fifteen

Skill Check

Add at least three transitions to the following passage. Use Tackling Transitions (handout) as a reference.

It is important for children to have responsibilities. Children need to learn how to complete different types of tasks. They need to learn that sharing responsibilities makes other people's lives easier. They need to understand that their skills are needed. They need to understand that everyone does things that they might not want to do. Children do need to have responsibilities.

Lesson Sixteen

Skill Check

Revise this sentence by moving the subject away from the beginning of the sentence. The subject of the sentence is underlined.

The <u>cat</u> was meowing loudly because it was hungry for its food.

Skill Checks (cont.)

Lesson Seventeen

Skill Check

Revise this passage by giving it a specific tone. To do this, identify the tone you want to create, and identify words that help describe and support the tone. Then, rewrite the passage using those words.

The house had white paint and black shutters. The inside was empty. There was a garden in the backyard.

Lesson Eighteen

Skill Check

Select a title for the passage below. Then, answer one of the following questions:

What technique did you use to help you select the title?
Why is the title you selected effective?

My dog's favorite activity is to go swimming in a lake. She loves it when I throw sticks in for her to chase. She swims out to the stick, grabs it, and brings it back to me. The only problem is, after she drops the stick in front of me, she shakes her wet fur and gets me all wet. Next time, I'm bringing an umbrella.

Lesson Nineteen

Skill Check

Describe a piece of writing you are currently working on, or recently completed. Select one of the following questions to answer:

How did you (or could you) choose to end the writing piece?
What techniques did you (or could you) use to help create the ending to your piece of writing?